Transportation

Preschool/Kindergarten

Save time and energy planning thematic units with this comprehensive resource. We've searched the 1990–1998 issues of **The MAILBOX®** and **Teacher's Helper®** magazines to find the best ideas for you to use when teaching a thematic unit about transportation. Included in this book are favorite units from the magazines, single ideas to extend a unit, and a variety of reproducible activities. Use these ready-to-roll activities to develop your own complete unit or simply to enhance your current lesson plans. You're sure to find everything you need for "wheel-ly" fun learning.

Editors:
Angie Kutzer
Thad H. McLaurin
Michele M. Stoffel Menzel

Artist:
Teresa R. Davidson

Cover Artist:
Kimberly Richard

www.themailbox.com

©2000 by THE EDUCATION CENTER, INC.
All rights reserved.
ISBN# 1-56234-351-3

Manufactured in the United States
10 9 8 7 6 5 4 3 2 1

Table Of Contents

Thematic Units...

Jackson

from The **MAILBOX**® magazine.

Tons Of Trucks

Vroom, vroom! Honk, honk! Get in gear with this truckload of learning activities. Your good buddies are sure to have tons of truckin' fun!

ideas by Lucia Kemp Henry

Let's Get Truckin'

Get your truck unit on the road by asking each youngster to bring in a toy truck or a magazine picture of a truck. During circle time, ask each youngster to describe the size and color of her truck or the truck in her picture. Help each child also brainstorm the kind of work for which her truck might be used. Use the toy trucks and pictures to help children identify similarities and differences in the trucks. Later assist small groups of children in sorting and classifying the trucks by type, size, and color. After each child has an opportunity to share her truck and sort the collection of trucks, display the toys on a table covered with a black, construction-paper road. Ask those youngsters who brought pictures to arrange and glue the pictures on a sheet of poster board or on a bulletin-board paper road.

A Song About My Truck

Follow up your circle-time sharing with this simple trucking song. Ask each youngster to think of two words that describe his truck. Sing the song below, replacing the words *big* and *shiny* with each child's chosen words.

(sung to the tune of "B-I-N-G-O")

Oh, look at my [big, shiny] truck!
I'm driving it today-o!
T-R-U-C-K
T-R-U-C-K
T-R-U-C-K
My truck is on its way-o!

Keep On Truckin'

Here's a song you can sing as you roll along. Each time you sing the song, replace the word *truckin'* with *drivin'*, *haulin'*, or *rollin'*. Encourage youngsters to develop their own movements for each verse.

(sung to the tune of "She'll Be Comin' 'Round the Mountain")

We'll be truckin' down the highway every day. Vroom! Vroom!
We'll be truckin' down the highway every day. Vroom! Vroom!
We'll be truckin' down the highway,
We'll be truckin' down the highway,
We'll be truckin' down the highway every day. Vroom! Vroom!

Up Close And Personal

Your preschoolers are sure to be fascinated with big trucks and their work. If possible watch some real trucks at work in your neighborhood. Or invite a truck driver to visit the school and give a tour of his own big rig. Whether or not you have the opportunity to check out real trucks, be sure to view the video *Close Up And Very Personal: Big Rigs* (available from Stage Fright Productions, 1-800-979-6800). Perfect for preschoolers, this video is all action with no narration. Your little ones will have the opportunity to fine-tune their listening skills and oral language as they hear, watch, and discuss how the big rigs hoot, honk, hiss, and roar.

Behind The Wheel

After watching the live action of a real truck or watching the suggested action video, give youngsters a chance to get their own big wheels in motion. Provide each child with her own big rig (chair). Encourage each student to imitate a truck's sounds and movements as she pretends to shut the door of her truck, buckle the seat belt, start the engine, turn on the lights, back up, honk the horn, turn on the windshield wipers, and drive away! After an appropriate length of time, direct your young drivers to put on the brakes and park at your own classroom truck stop for a snack and maybe a rest.

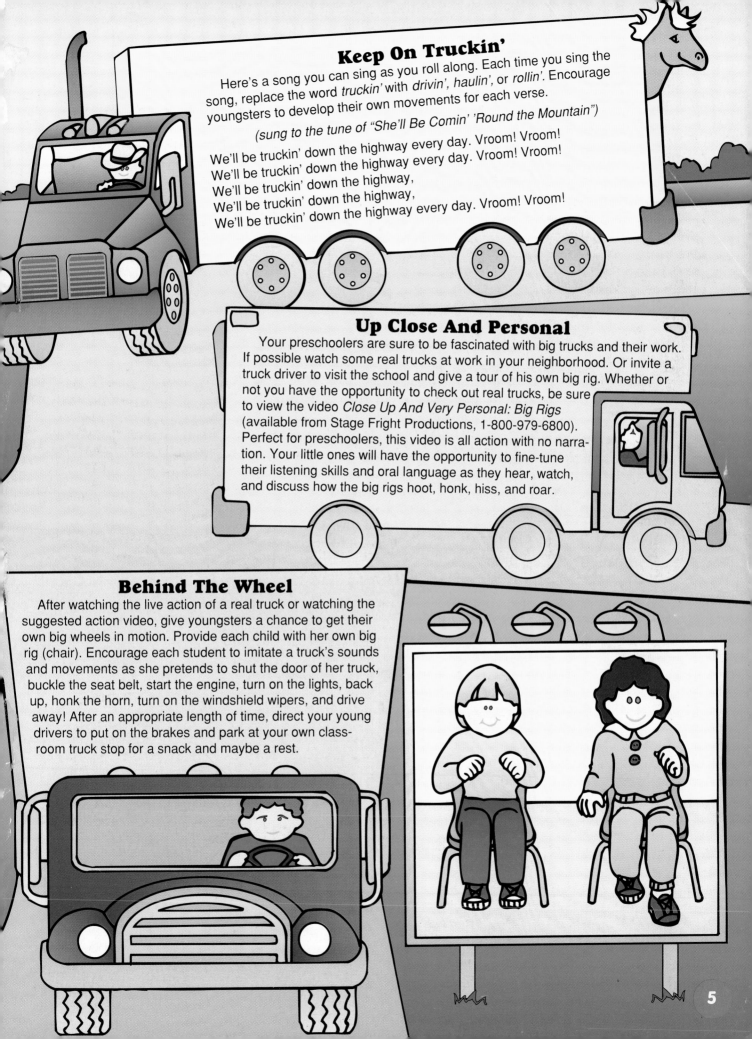

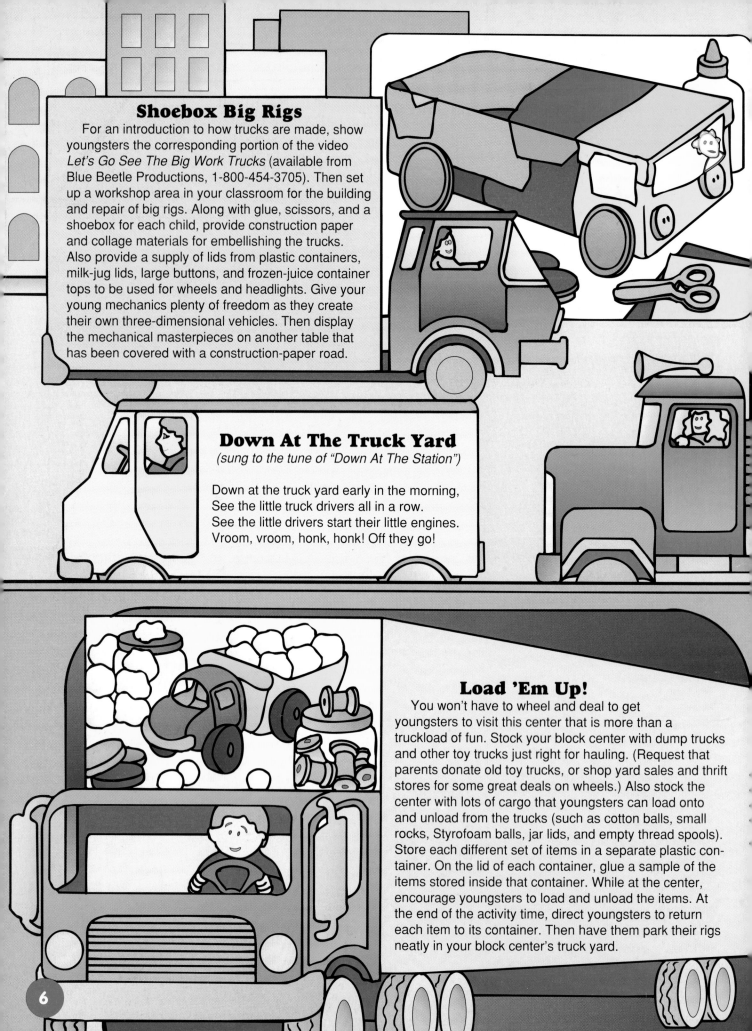

Shoebox Big Rigs

For an introduction to how trucks are made, show youngsters the corresponding portion of the video *Let's Go See The Big Work Trucks* (available from Blue Beetle Productions, 1-800-454-3705). Then set up a workshop area in your classroom for the building and repair of big rigs. Along with glue, scissors, and a shoebox for each child, provide construction paper and collage materials for embellishing the trucks. Also provide a supply of lids from plastic containers, milk-jug lids, large buttons, and frozen-juice container tops to be used for wheels and headlights. Give your young mechanics plenty of freedom as they create their own three-dimensional vehicles. Then display the mechanical masterpieces on another table that has been covered with a construction-paper road.

Down At The Truck Yard
(sung to the tune of "Down At The Station")

Down at the truck yard early in the morning,
See the little truck drivers all in a row.
See the little drivers start their little engines.
Vroom, vroom, honk, honk! Off they go!

Load 'Em Up!

You won't have to wheel and deal to get youngsters to visit this center that is more than a truckload of fun. Stock your block center with dump trucks and other toy trucks just right for hauling. (Request that parents donate old toy trucks, or shop yard sales and thrift stores for some great deals on wheels.) Also stock the center with lots of cargo that youngsters can load onto and unload from the trucks (such as cotton balls, small rocks, Styrofoam balls, jar lids, and empty thread spools). Store each different set of items in a separate plastic container. On the lid of each container, glue a sample of the items stored inside that container. While at the center, encourage youngsters to load and unload the items. At the end of the activity time, direct youngsters to return each item to its container. Then have them park their rigs neatly in your block center's truck yard.

Big Wheels Big Book

Your big-wheel watchers will want to look at and read this class big book over and over again. Enlarge and duplicate a dump truck pattern or a flatbed truck pattern (page 9) for each child. Cut out each truck pattern and glue it to a large sheet of light-colored construction paper. Gather a supply of shaped sponges and pour different colors of paint into pie pans. Instruct each child to select a sponge, dip it in paint, and press it onto her paper so that the truck appears to carry a load. When the paintings are dry, ask each child to dictate a sentence about her truck's load. Write each child's sentence on her page. Laminate the pages if desired; then bind them between titled pages. Send the class publication home for youngsters to share with their families.

Samantha's truck carries pumpkins.

Five Little Trucks

Teach this truck fingerplay to reinforce the basic colors and counting from one to five. In advance, duplicate the truck patterns (page 9) onto white construction paper; then color each numbered truck as indicated in the poem. Laminate the truck patterns; then cut on the bold lines. Back each truck pattern with felt. Use the truck patterns to accompany the poem "Five Little Trucks."

Five little trucks drive down the road.
Five little trucks each carry a load.

The **blue** truck is number **one**.
This truck can carry a ton!

The **red** truck is number **two**.
This truck can carry you!

The **yellow** truck is number **three**.
This truck can carry a tree.

The **green** truck is number **four**.
This truck can carry much more!

The **orange** truck is number **five**.
This truck is fun to drive!

—*Lucia Kemp Henry*

Trucks, Trucks, And More Trucks

If your youngsters are really on a roll learning about trucks, try these additional uses for the patterns on page 9.

• To make individual truck-shaped books, enlarge and duplicate any of the truck patterns. Staple each truck pattern to a supply of blank paper that has been cut to match the size or shape of the pattern. On the blank pages, encourage youngsters to attach truck stickers, glue magazine pictures of trucks, or draw pictures of their favorite trucks.

• Duplicate the set of patterns onto several different colors of construction paper. Laminate the truck patterns; then cut on the bold lines. Encourage youngsters to sort the trucks into groups by color or type.

• To create three or more different-sized trucks, reduce and enlarge one type of truck several times. Encourage youngsters to arrange the trucks by size.

• Use your choice of truck patterns to create nametags or to label students' truck projects.

On The Road Again

Give this art idea a ride and you'll arrive at the destination of a delightful display. Using books about trucks (see the suggestions below), show students pictures of the side view of a truck. Then provide each child with a large sheet of white construction paper and a supply of colorful, precut, construction-paper shapes including different sizes of circles, squares, rectangles, and triangles. Ask each child to arrange the shapes of his choice to create a truck on the paper. Assist each child in gluing his arranged shapes on the paper. When the glue is dry, cut around the overall shape of each truck. Mount the projects on a bulletin board along with paper roads and road signs. Way to go!

On The Move

Grease your wheels and start your engines! Youngsters are sure to enjoy moving to this action poem about the parts of a truck.

Here is the tractor so big and strong.	*Stand on toes and flex arm muscles.*
Here is the trailer so wide and long.	*Stretch arms out very wide.*
Here is the cab where the driver will be.	*Pretend to sit in driver's seat.*
Here is the window so the driver can see.	*Pretend to look out a window.*
Here is the steering wheel that's round.	*Pretend to steer.*
Here are the tires that roll on the ground.	*Make a rolling motion with arms.*
Here is the load that the truck will take.	*Pretend to hold a big box.*
Here is the engine that can roar and shake.	*Wiggle body and make engine noise.*
Here is the truck that's on its way;	*Pretend to drive.*
Off to work for another day.	*Wave good-bye.*

—Lucia Kemp Henry

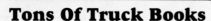

Tons Of Truck Books

Truck
Written & Illustrated by Donald Crews
Published by Puffin Books

Trucks
Written & Illustrated by Byron Barton
Published by HarperCollins Children's Books

Trucks
Written & Illustrated by Anne F. Rockwell
Published by Dutton Children's Books

Trucks
Written & Illustrated by Gail Gibbons
Published by HarperCollins Children's Books

Truck Song
Written by Diane Siebert
Illustrated by Byron Barton
Published by HarperCollins Children's Books

Sam Goes Trucking
Written & Photographed by Henry Horenstein
Published by Houghton Mifflin Company

Eye Openers: Trucks
A Dorling Kindersley Book
Published by Aladdin Books

The Dump Truck
Written by Arlene Blanchard
Illustrated by Tony Wells
Published by Candlewick Press

Trucks Trucks Trucks
Written & Illustrated by Peter Sis
Published by Greenwillow Books

Mighty Machines: Truck
Written by Claire Llewellyn
Published by Dorling Kindersley

Truck Patterns

Use with "Five Little Trucks," "Big Wheels Big Book," and "Trucks, Trucks, And More Trucks" on page 7.

1. Dump truck
2. Pickup truck
3. Flatbed truck
4. Panel truck
5. Child's truck

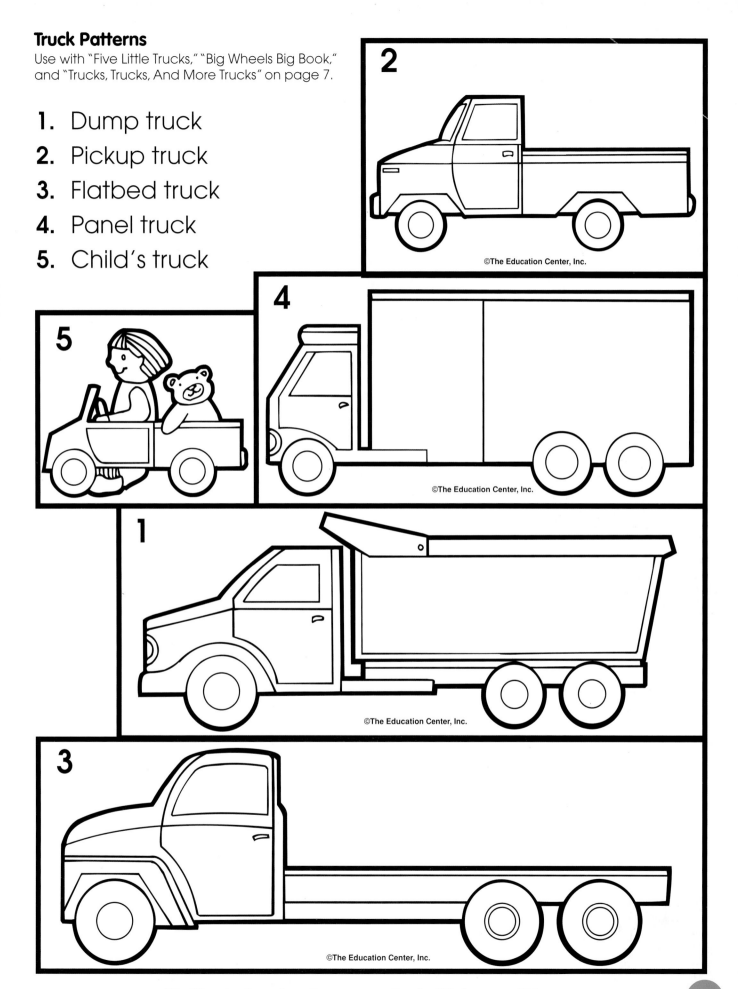

©The Education Center, Inc.

©The Education Center, Inc.

©The Education Center, Inc.

©The Education Center, Inc.

Traveling

Whether your youngsters are experienced travelers by land, air, sea, or pure imagination; they're bound to find fun and adventure in this traveling unit. As you read together, youngsters will be accompanied by an assorted crew of characters to places both real and imaginary. So gather this collection of children's literature and set your itinerary for a delightful venture across the curriculum.

*introduction, reviews, and ideas by
Anne Bustard and Mackie Rhodes*

*Note to the teacher: All of the books featured in this unit were in print at the time the original magazine was published. We've taken care to choose featured books that are currently in print, but we cannot guarantee that every book featured will remain in print. Should you have trouble locating any of these titles, please check with your media specialist.

Art by Marilyn G. Barr

Arthur's Family Vacation
By Marc Brown
Published by Little, Brown And Company; 1993

Rain, rain, go away! The family's beach vacation is almost a complete washout until Arthur steps in to save the day. A perfectly sunny read.

Share this story; then invite students to share their own experiences with rained-out travel plans. Afterward have students brainstorm a list of rainy day activities. Invite each child to secretly illustrate one of these activities or an activity of her own choosing. Then write each child's whispered dictation about her drawing on the back of her paper. Have each child, in turn, show her illustration to the class. Encourage the other students to question the illustrator with yes/no questions until the pictured activity is identified. To extend this idea, invite youngsters to participate in activities from the list when they are greeted by rainy school days.

Just Us Women
By Jeannette Caines
Illustrated by Pat Cummings
Published by Harper & Row, Publishers, Inc.; 1982

The fun is in the planning! A young girl and her aunt dream of all the fun and flexibility they'll have as jump-off time for their women-only road trip approaches.

The girl in this story plans to take pictures to record her travel events. To extend this story, invite each child to create a camera from a small box and an assortment of craft items, such as buttons, bottle caps, construction paper, and yarn. Give each child a paper strip divided into three equal sections to represent film. Then guide your class on a trip around your school, inviting each child to "snap" three photos with her camera. Have each child sketch a simple picture of each subject on a different section of her film. Back in the classroom, invite her to "develop" her film by illustrating each film section on a half-sheet of paper. Then have the child mount each picture on a black sheet of construction paper. Bind all the pages into a photo album titled "Our Class Trip"; then have each student share her page with the class.

Hannah And Jack
By Mary Nethery
Illustrated by Mary Morgan
Published by Atheneum Books For Young Readers, 1996

While Hannah visits Grandma, she gathers gifts and sends postcards home to her much-missed cat, Jack. And when she returns home, she hosts a Glad-To-Be-Back Party for her favorite feline friend. "Purr-fectly" satisfying!

To extend this story, invite youngsters to create their own puzzle postcards. Ask each child to imagine he is traveling away from home. Invite him to create a postcard by illustrating a large blank index card with one of his imaginary vacation spots. Then have him puzzle-cut his card into six to eight pieces. Instruct student pairs to exchange and complete each other's puzzles. After each child has assembled his partner's puzzle, have each creator tell about his picture. Invite youngsters to switch partners and repeat the activity. Afterward encourage each child to take his puzzle home in an envelope to share with his family.

I Fly
By Anne Rockwell
Illustrated by Annette Cable
Published by Crown Publishers, Inc.; 1997

Join a young boy as he shares the sights, sounds, and sensations of flying. As the plane flies up, into and above the clouds, then back down again, the boy's enthusiasm about flying remains elevated. What a high-flying adventure!

After sharing this youngster's flying experiences with your class, invite students to imagine a high-flying adventure of their own. Have students close their eyes and imagine they are on an airplane. Give a narrative of the plane's taxi and liftoff. Continue narrating the plane's ascent through and above the clouds, encouraging youngsters to imagine the sights they might see while flying so high. Then narrate the plane's descent and landing. Afterward ask each child to illustrate a sight he might have seen while flying. Help him staple a sheet of thin, rolled batting over his drawing to represent clouds. Then encourage each child to share his cloud-covered picture with the class.

Dinosaurs Travel: A Guide For Families On The Go

By Laurie Krasny Brown and Marc Brown
Published by Little, Brown and Company; 1988

These adventuresome dinosaurs provide practical tips on everything youngsters need to know about traveling—from planning and preparing for a trip to the return back home. A must-read before setting out on any journey.

Using the book as a prompt, challenge students to name many different ways people might travel. Then create a travel graph by labeling each suggested mode of transportation across a length of bulletin board paper. Ask each child to write his name on a different sticky note to represent each type of transportation he has used. Then have the child attach his name under each applicable category. As a class, use the graph to determine which modes of transportation are most and least used by students. Then invite each youngster to tell the class about one of his traveling adventures.

Tell youngsters that many people keep a journal when they are traveling. Have each child design a construction-paper cover titled "My Travel Journal." On separate sheets of paper, have the student record a real or an imaginary travel experience corresponding to each type of transportation on the graph. Help her attach her pages to her journal cover with a metal ring. Encourage each student to add to her journal as she travels in different ways and to different places in the future. Periodically invite youngsters to share their journal entries with the class.

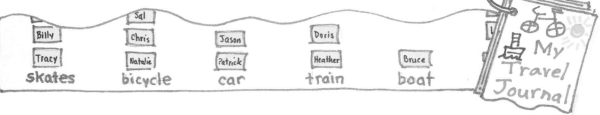

The Best Vacation Ever

By Stuart J. Murphy
Illustrated by Nadine Bernard Westcott
Published by HarperCollins Publishers, Inc.; 1997

A simple survey of each person's preferences helps a family decide on the best vacation spot ever. Use this delightful story to teach youngsters how to record information on charts as well as use the results for decision making.

This story leads right into decision-making practice in class. Have each member of a small group prepare a chart similar to the one on page 15 of the book. Instruct the students in the group to decide which category each member's chart will represent; then label the charts. Perhaps they'd like to choose categories from the book (weather, distance, etc.) or child-generated categories, such as transportation and accommodations. Have each student record his group members' preferences on his chart. Ask each group to discuss the results of their charts, then decide on a real or an imaginary place that meets the majority of the group's preferences. Invite a spokesperson to present his group's results and decision to the class.

The Bag I'm Taking To Grandma's

By Shirley Neitzel
Illustrated by Nancy Winslow Parker
Published by Greenwillow Books, 1995

Bag some fun with this cumulative, rhyming, rebus story. In this tale, a young boy sets about packing his favorite things to take to Grandma's—until he discovers his mother has another plan.

Extend this story by encouraging each child to pack for her own trip to a relative's house. For each student, cut off one large panel and the bottom of a paper grocery bag. After reading the story, give each child three sheets of construction paper. Have her label the top of each page with "Clothes," "Toys," or "Food." On each page, ask her to glue corresponding magazine cutouts of things she might pack for her trip. Stack and staple the pages to the large panel. Then have the child glue a yarn handle to the top of the bag. Ask the child to write or dictate a title such as "The Bag I'm Taking To [Place]" on another sheet of paper. Then have her glue the title to the bag as shown. As each child shares her bag book, invite her to explain why she "packed" each item.

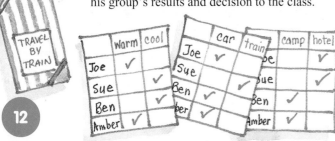

Away From Home
By Anita Lobel
Published by Greenwillow Books, 1994

The world is a stage and boys are the stars in this alliterative alphabetic travelogue from Amsterdam to Zaandam. A guide to the 26 sites highlighted in this pictorial delight is included at the end of the book.

Whether youngsters are world travelers or home-bodies, they will enjoy creating their own alphabetical stage sets with this idea. Assign each child a different letter; then have him illustrate a sheet of unlined chart paper with a place that begins with that letter. The drawing might represent a local, a foreign, or an imaginary place. Write the child's dictated alliterative sentence about his illustration at the bottom of his page. Sequence and display the scenes in a hallway for viewing by students, teachers, and school visitors.

Explain to students that travelers need passports to enter other countries. Help them to identify which sites in the book are found in countries other than the United States. Then have each child create her own passport. To do this, stack one half sheet of paper onto a half sheet of blue construction paper. Fold the stack in half, book-style; then staple the pages together along the fold. Print "Passport" on the front cover with a gold crayon or marker. Ask the child to write her first and last names on the first page, her address on the second page, and her phone number on the third page. On the last page, instruct her to create a self-portrait. Encourage youngsters to use their passports as they role-play travelers journeying to different countries.

My Little Island
By Frané Lessac
Published by J. B. Lippincott, 1984

As a young boy travels back to the Caribbean island of his birth, the sights and sounds of the island come alive through his accounts of his visit. Bright, bold illustrations make this a fanciful favorite.

Almost everywhere the boy travels on his island, calypso and reggae music is heard. The heartbeat of this music comes from steel drums. Ask your school's cafeteria manager to set aside several large cans. Wash each can and line the rim with vinyl tape to cover all sharp edges. Invite small groups to use bold colors of paint pens to decorate each can. After the paint dries, invite small groups of drummers, in turn, to beat their drums to reggae music or other music with a moving drum-beat. Then encourage youngsters to create their own rhythms as their classmates dance to the rhythm of the beat.

Abuela
By Arthur Dorros
Illustrated by Elisa Kleven
Published by Dutton Children's Books, 1991

Fly with Rosalba on an imaginary trip with her grandmother—her abuela—*through the skies over New York City. The pair's adventures will entice even the most reluctant traveler to journey into his imagination.*

After sharing this delightful journey with youngsters, invite them to take an imaginary flight over their own town. Ask them to name some of the sights they might view from the air. Where would they like to stop and visit during their journey? Perhaps relatives' homes? Or the park? Then ask each child to fill a large sheet of construction paper with an illustration of himself flying like Abuela. Have him cut loosely around his drawing, then trace around that cutout on several additional sheets of construction paper. After the child cuts out these outlines, encourage him to illustrate each cutout with a sight from his imaginary flight. Then have him stack and staple his pages behind his self-illustration. Invite him to share his book and imaginary travels with the class.

Kate Heads West
By Pat Brisson
Illustrated by Rick Brown
Published by Bradbury Press, 1990

Round up youngsters for a four-state journey through the West as Kate shares her vacation experiences in letter form. Visits to the Johnson Space Center, Carlsbad Caverns, and the Petrified Forest are included.

Display a map of the United States as you read this story, pointing out each location that Kate visits. Then write each of the four states across the top of a sheet of chart paper. Have youngsters list each site Kate visited under the corresponding state. After reviewing the sites with youngsters, ask them to decide which of the states they would most like to visit. Why? Then invite them to imagine themselves at their preferred sites. Have each child illustrate his choice on a sheet of paper labeled with "I would visit the state of _____ to see _____."
Help him fill in the blanks; then encourage him to share his illustration with the class.

Three Days On A River In A Red Canoe
By Vera B. Williams
Published by Greenwillow Books, 1981

The purchase of a used red canoe is the start of an eventful river adventure for four travelers.

Share this story with students; then set up a real canoe (or an inflated raft) along with additional props, such as oars, life jackets, small camp equipment, sleeping bags, and fishing poles. Ask each group of up to four students to locate a river on a map of your state. Encourage the group to plot its path along the river and to plan where it will stop for meals and two overnight stays. Then invite the group to role-play its travels down the river. After the imaginary journey, have the group members create a journal and/or picture album of their river trip to share with the class.

Kate On The Coast
By Pat Brisson
Illustrated by Rick Brown
Published by Bradbury Press, 1992

Kate's on the move again! After relocating with her family to Seattle, Washington, Kate shares her travel adventures to her new city as well as to Alaska, Canada, California, Oregon, and Hawaii.

Extend this story with a game of Travel Lotto. To prepare, duplicate the lotto cards and gameboard (page 15) for each child, plus one extra card set. Have each child color and cut out his lotto cards, then glue the cards onto his gameboard. Prepare the extra card set to serve as caller cards; then appoint a Caller. As each card is called, each player covers the corresponding picture on his gamecard with a bean counter. (If desired, ask youngsters to recall where each item was seen by Kate.) The first player to cover all his cards becomes the Caller for the next round of play.

Pigs Ahoy!
By David McPhail
Published by Dutton Children's Books, 1995

A traveler's peaceful vacation is abruptly interrupted by several swine as a cruise is turned into a captain's nightmare. This might just be the carnival of all cruises!

After discussing the different events in this story, challenge students to create their own version of *Pigs Ahoy!* To begin, list as many cruise-related words as possible on a sheet of chart paper. Have youngsters brainstorm rhyming words for each listed word. Then have each child use the list as a guide to create, then illustrate, a rhyming statement about pigs on a boat. Stack and bind the pages between two construction-paper covers shaped like a cruise ship; then title the class book "Pigs Ahoy!" During a reading of the book, invite each child to share his page with the class.

Travel Lotto

THE WAGON TRAIL

Load a day's worth of fun into little red wagons and head outside. A day on the wagon trail is all you'll need to get things rollin'!

WAGONS HO!

Find out which students in your class have wagons. Request that parents bring the wagons to school in advance of wagon day. When you are sure of the number of wagons you'll have, use these ideas to fill each wagon with the materials needed for independent play as well as teacher-directed activities. Consider asking for parent volunteers for your wagon day so that you'll have adult supervision at each station.

Once you've prepared the wagons, take them outside and arrange them in a circle. Based on the number of wagon stations you'll have on your wagon trail, divide the class into groups. Assign each group a station; then rotate the groups throughout the day. Wagons ho!

SPINNING YOUR WHEELS

In advance of wagon day, have each child bring to school toys that have wheels. (Be sure to label each toy with the owner's name.) Place the toys in a wagon. Encourage children at this station to discuss the similarities and differences in the toys. If desired fill the wagon with sand or soil.

Eva Murdock—Preschool
Children's Center, Shenandoah Baptist
 Church
Roanoke, VA

READING ABOUT WHEELS

Fill a wagon full of transportation-related titles. Encourage youngsters to find pictures of vehicles with wheels. Be sure to bring these great titles along for the ride!

The Big Book Of Things That Go
A Dorling Kindersley Book
Published by Dorling Kindersley
 Publishing, Inc.

On The Go
Written by Ann Morris
Photographed by Ken Heyman
Published by Mulberry Books

Big Wheels
Written and Illustrated by
 Anne Rockwell
(Check your library)

Wheels
Written and Illustrated by
 Byron Barten
(Check your library)

MEALS ON WHEELS

How about snacks on wheels? Encourage youngsters to roll on over to this station to make edible wagons. For each child you will need one graham cracker broken in half lengthwise; four 1/2" thick, unpeeled banana slices; two toothpicks; several animal crackers; peanut butter; and a plastic knife. To make an edible wagon, spread peanut butter on both halves of the graham cracker. Secure a banana slice on each end of both toothpicks. Place the banana wheels and toothpick axles atop one peanut-butter covered graham cracker. Press the second graham cracker atop the first, so that the peanut butter is facing up. Press animal crackers into the peanut butter. Wow! It's an edible animal wagon!

Eva Murdock—Preschool
Children's Center, Shenandoah Baptist
   Church
Roanoke, VA

WATER WHEELS

Water play will add a cool touch to your outdoor wagon day. Fill a wagon with water and provide water wheels for exploration. Also include toy paddle boats and egg beaters for extra fun. Keep some towels nearby. The fun is sure to be wet and wild!

A WAGON OF MY OWN

To make a toy wagon of her own, each child will need one small shoebox, four wheels cut from black poster board, four large brads, one 12" pipe cleaner, red tempera paint, and a paintbrush. Prepare this station for painting by spreading newspaper inside the real wagon. To make a toy wagon, direct each child to paint her shoebox. When the paint is dry, assist her in attaching the wheels to the box with the brads. Poke two small holes in one end of the box. Thread one end of the pipe cleaner through both holes; then twist the pipe cleaner to secure it. Twist and shape the opposite end of the pipe cleaner so that it resembles a handle. These wagons really roll!

HAVE A BALL

Fill a wagon with a supply of small balls (or beanbags) in a variety of colors. Encourage the children to throw the balls into the wagon, count as they fill the wagon with balls, and sort the balls by color.

JOIN THE BANDWAGON

Stock a wagon station with rhythm instruments, a battery-operated tape player, and audiotapes of lively music. Sounds like wagon fun has begun!

IN AND OUT

This interactive station offers practice with locational concepts and opposites while encouraging language development. Place as many teddy bears or stuffed toys in the wagon as you will have children visiting the station at one time. When a group arrives at the station, give each child a toy to hold. Then read aloud *Sam's Wagon* by Barbro Lindgren (William Morrow and Company). As a follow-up, instruct each child in turn to place his toy inside, outside, under, and beside the wagon. Encourage each child to explain where his toy is located in relationship to the wagon. Next have pairs of children demonstrate opposite locations such as in and out, or over and under the wagon. Culminate the activity by inviting each child in turn to get in the wagon with his toy and go for a wagon ride. Wheee!

Kathy Mulvihill—Four-Year-Olds
Wee Care Preschool
Allendale, MI

BUILDING BLOCKS

A wagon makes the perfect foundation for a tower. As each group visits this station, encourage the children to cooperatively build a tower or building. When the group's structure is complete, carefully wheel it around the wagon trail for everyone to admire. Or, if your trail is bumpy, take a picture of each group of children with their structure.

COVERED WAGONS

Isn't it the perfect time of year for a parade? Culminate your day by returning the materials in each wagon to the classroom. Wash and dry any wagons containing sand and water. Then return the wagons to the trail. Provide youngsters with a collection of construction paper, markers, streamers, and cloth scraps. Encourage them to decorate the wagons by taping or tying on materials as desired. Then load everyone into the wagons, provide noisemakers, and head off on a wagon day parade.

Beauie Withrow—Pre-K Special Needs
E. M. Yoder Elementary
Mebane, NC

Rolling Along

Enhance your transportation unit with this booklet idea. Using a black crayon, have each child color the outer portion of a paper plate. Then add the open sentence, "A _____ can go," and his name. Have him complete the sentence by illustrating a wheel-related form of transportation. To make a front cover for the booklet, decorate a paper plate as shown. Use another plate for the back cover; then insert the completed pages between the covers. Punch holes near the tops of the plates, join them with a metal ring, and you're ready to roll!

Vicki Sherman
Central Elementary School
Centerville, IA

Ready To Roll
by Mrs. Sherman's Class

A [car] can go.
Tyler

Car Wash

Turn your waterplay table into a car wash for the day. Include sponges, gentle liquid cleanser, and a few toy cars. To give your car wash a musical lift, teach your youngsters the song that follows:

(sung to the tune of "The Oscar Mayer® Weiner Theme Song")

Oh, I really like to give a car a car wash.
Squirting, soaping, scrubbing dirt away!
Oh, I really like to give a car a car wash.
Why, I could sing and scrub away the day!

Betty Silkunas
Lansdale, PA

Colorful Sidewalks

Here's an outdoor idea that's really "write" on! Gather your toy cars and trucks and a supply of sidewalk chalk. Take youngsters outside to a concrete area such as a sidewalk. Using the chalk have the class cooperatively draw roads, houses, and buildings on the concrete. Then have students "drive" their vehicles on the chalk roadways. Beep, beep!

Elaine M. Utt—Two-Year-Olds
La Petite Academy
Tampa, FL

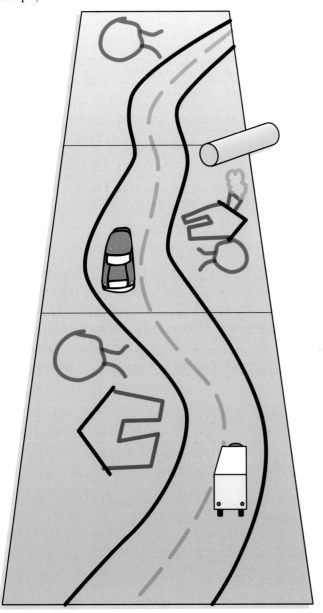

On The Move

You won't have to be a wheeler-dealer to get youngsters excited about this outdoor activity. During a transportation unit, designate a day as Vehicle Day. Invite each child to bring a vehicle—a bike, tricycle, etc.—to school on that day. (Arrange to have extra vehicles for children who may not have brought one.) As each child arrives at school with his vehicle, ask him to park it outside your door. Inside the classroom, show the class a real license plate. Then have each child make his own plate by tracing and coloring numerals onto a tagboard rectangle. Punch holes in the top of each plate; then thread it with a length of heavy yarn. Assist each child in tying his license plate to his vehicle. Encourage the children to ride their registered vehicles on a paved area outside. Beep, beep! Honk, honk! Here we go!

Sue Lewis Lein
St. Pius X
Wauwatosa, WI

Musical Cars

Honk, honk! Rattle, rattle, rattle. Crash. Beep, beep! This motorized version of musical chairs is versatile enough to teach youngsters colors, numeral or letter recognition, and social skills. To prepare for a game of musical cars, cut pairs of car shapes from different colors of poster board or laminated construction paper. Label each pair with a numeral or letter; then tape them together at the top only. For each different color of car, cut a matching circle to resemble a steering wheel. Label each wheel with a letter or numeral to correspond with those written on the cars.

To play, arrange as many chairs in a circle as you have children. Slip the cars over the backs of the chairs. Provide each child with a steering wheel. Direct the group to "drive" around the cars as you play music. When the music stops, have each child match either the color of his steering wheel or the letter or numeral on his steering wheel to a car. If more than one child matches a car, encourage youngsters to carpool by sharing the seat.

adapted from an idea by Laurie Curti—Three-, Four-, And Five-Year-Olds With Communication Disorders
Sutherland Elementary, Palm Harbor, FL

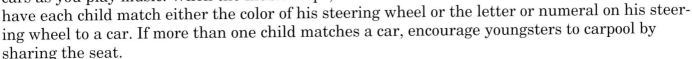

Heavy Traffic

Start your engines! This activity is sure to keep traffic moving in your classroom. Provide each child with a cardboard pizza or cake base to serve as a steering wheel. Encourage youngsters to move about your room as you read the following poem. For added fun, pair youngsters. Give one child a steering wheel and ask the second child to put his hands on his partner's shoulders. Direct the first child to steer as the second child moves along with him.

I'm a bright and shiny car,
So beautiful to see.
I certainly don't want to crash
And get a scratch on me.

As I travel down the road,
I'm careful not to bump.
I drive around the other cars
And never go "kerthump"!

Dr. Grace Morris
Southwest Texas State University
San Marcos, TX

Boats Afloat

Invite youngsters to cruise into creativity as they explore the boat-making possibilities at your water table. Prepare a boat-builders workshop that includes pictures of boats and these items: cardboard tubes, margarine tubs, Ivory® Soap bars, foam meat trays (*Ask your grocer for a class supply of unused meat trays.*), milk cartons, foam egg cartons, sponges, straws, rubber bands, construction paper, scissors, tape, clay, toothpicks, yarn, a hole puncher, crayons, and craft sticks. Encourage youngsters to experiment—even to sink a few ships—until they make some boats that float. Need navigation? Here are some suggestions:

Tube Raft—Rubber-band two or more cardboard tubes together to create a raft.

Margarine-Tub Sailboat—Press a ball of clay in the bottom of a margarine tub. Insert a straw in the clay; then tape a decorated paper sail to the straw.

Soap Boat—Attach a decorated paper sail to one end of a craft stick. Insert the other end of the craft stick into the top of the bar of soap.

Egg-Cup Boats—Cut apart the individual cups of a foam egg carton. Float the cups in the water.

Meat-Tray Barges—Punch a hole in opposite ends of each of several foam meat trays. Connect the trays with yarn to make a barge.

Lori Kent
Hood River, OR

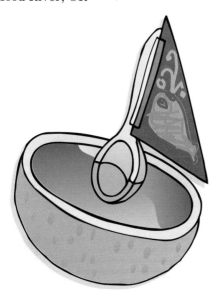

Shipshape Snacks

When your sailors get hungry, have them dock at your classroom cooking center to make some shipshape snacks. In advance cut ten navel oranges in half. Remove the pulp and squeeze the juice from the orange halves; then place them on a tray. Follow the directions on a three-ounce package for preparing blue, berry-flavored gelatin. Pour the gelatin into the orange halves; then place the halves in the refrigerator for at least four hours. To make a snack, a child uses markers to decorate a construction-paper triangle. He then tapes the triangle to the handle of a plastic spoon before inserting the spoon into the gelatin. "Tummy-ho!"

Sailing
Sail into windy seas with this nifty nautical rhyme.

This is a sail.

This is the boat.

Upon the ocean,

It will float.

And when a big, strong wind does blow,

Around the ocean the boat will go.

—Marie E. Cecchini

Row Your Boat

Ahoy, mateys! Make the most of your transportation theme by creating a boat for use in your dramatic play area. Cut the top or side from a large box; then cut out a few portholes. Use the leftover cardboard to make a sturdy steering wheel and an anchor. Then have little ones help you paint the boat with a bright color of tempera paint. Add some oceangoing props such as a life jacket, a tackle box, and some wooden dowels with strings attached to serve as fishing poles. Then encourage youngsters to set sail into the sea of imagination!

Jennifer Liptak—Three-Year-Olds
Building Blocks Of Learning, Denville, NJ

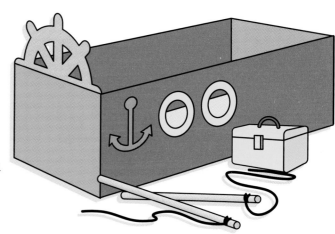

Sink The Boat!

Here's an activity that mixes literature, science, and a little math. Read aloud *Who Sank The Boat?* by Pamela Allen. After discussing the book, provide each small group of children with a water-filled container (such as a large bowl), a supply of metal washers, and a small "boat"—a block of wood into which you have partially driven two straight nails. Have each group float their boat in the water. In turn, have children place washers on the nails. Encourage youngsters to make hypotheses and draw conclusions about the role weight plays in regard to sinking and floating objects.

Cheryl Fischer—Gr. K, Remsen-Union Elementary, Remsen, IA

Circle-Time Travels

Take each youngster on a journey in which his imagination is his guide. Have students sit in a circle. Provide each child with a plastic plate. Have him hold the plate and pretend that it's a steering wheel. Then tell students that they will be going on imaginary vacations. Ask a student volunteer to give a vacation destination—such as Grandmother's house or the beach—and a mode of transportation—such as a car or train. As the children steer their vehicles, encourage them to tell about the people, places, and things they see on their trip. After this trip has been completed, ask another volunteer to make the next destination and transportation suggestion. Off we go!

Glenda C. Roddey, An Academe For Children, Inc., Springdale, AR

Gone Four-Wheelin'

To create perfect conditions for winter driving, squirt mounds of shaving cream into an empty water table. Your little ones will love plowing through the snow with toy vehicles to get to their imagined destinations. There's "snow" telling what will occur in this blizzard of activity.

Joan Banker—Three- And Four-Year-Olds
St. Mary's Child Development Center
Garner, NC

Transportation Trendsetters

Put youngsters' creative-thinking skills in gear at this transportation center. Stock the center with a large box filled with an assortment of items (such as plastic bottles, tissue rolls, bottle caps, plastic lids, buttons, straws, etc.), glue, tape, and string. A student uses the materials in the center to create an original form of transportation. Label each child's creation with his name and the name of his vehicle; then add it to a classroom display. Vrrrroom!

Mary Begley—Gr. K
St. Charles Primary
Chippewa Falls, WI

Blake's Bottlemobile

Extend that catchy "Bus Song" into a language activity! Mount a large bus cutout on a board. Have children color and cut out illustrations of people or things to be mounted in or on the bus. Write each youngster's dictation on a construction-paper speech balloon; then display it near his illustration. You're sure to hear compliments on this board all around the school.

Vicki Altland—Gr. K, Florence Mattison Elementary, Conway, AR

Traffic Light-Ups

Ingredients:
1 graham cracker for every four children
peanut butter
1 each of red, yellow, and green candy-
    coated chocolate pieces per child

Utensils And Supplies:
napkin
1 plastic knife per child

Teacher Preparation:
    Break each cracker into its four sections. Arrange the ingredients and utensils near the step-by-step direction cards (page 27). For a fun fingerplay tie-in, see page 28.

Diane Leschak-Halverson—Three-, Four-, And Five-Year-Olds
Nashwauk-Keewatin ECFE, Keewatin, MN

Stop And Go

Teach your youngsters a little traffic safety using this catchy verse. Then rev up their engines with the traffic-light treats described on page 26.

Red on top

Means stop.

Yellow in between:

Stay and wait for green.

Green below:

Let's go!

Diane Leschak-Halverson

Scraping The Sky

Balance your transportation landscape with a city skyscraper. Have students paint an appliance box black or dark gray. Then have them attach aluminum-foil rectangles to two sides for windows. From another side, cut a door. On the remaining side, have youngsters glue pictures of outdoor city scenes. (Travel agents are good sources for such pictures.) On the inside of the box, have them glue pictures of indoor city scenes. Then convert a box into a taxi to be parked near the skyscraper. Store transportation-related books inside the sky-scraper and the cab.

Floor Display

Are you looking around for places to display student artwork? Look down and try the floor! If desired, attach a picture of each child to her work. Then laminate each piece of artwork and tape it to the floor with clear packing tape. Add complementary theme-related details to the floor for extra fun. For example, with transportation-related artwork, include a construction-paper road.

Diann M. Kroos—Preschool, SRI/St. Elizabeth Child Development Center, Lincoln, NE

Start Your Engines

Your children will zoom over to this magnetic raceway to practice hand/eye coordination. Draw and color a racetrack on a large piece of tagboard. Then draw, color, and cut out several car outlines from tagboard. Laminate the track and the cars. Slide a large paper clip onto each car. Tape the ends of the tagboard raceway to the edges of two tables so that the track is suspended in air. Place the cars on the track. Invite a child to use the raceway by moving a magnet underneath the tagboard. On your mark, get set, go!

Kim Richman—Preschool
The Learning Zone, Des Moines, IA

Track And Wash

Add a new twist to an old favorite art activity. Pour a thin layer of tempera paint in each of several shallow pans, using a different color in each pan. Roll a toy car through a pan of paint and then "drive" it all over a sheet of art paper or a length of bulletin-board paper. Repeat this with another toy vehicle or two. When each of your students has participated in this art experience, set up a tub of soapy water and have students take turns manning this mock car wash. Don't be surprised if your youngsters enjoy the cleanup more than the art.

Joann E. Lukasiewicz—Preschool
Visually Impaired Preschool, Buffalo, NY

Tabletop Town

Enhance your block area with a tabletop town cut from felt. Begin by cutting a large piece of felt to fit on a tabletop. Cut additional colors of felt into strips to create a maze of roads that can be placed on the larger piece of felt. Also cut out felt trees, houses, and other buildings if desired. Decorate the felt pieces with slick or puffy fabric paint. Little ones will love setting up the town and driving toy cars and trucks along its roadways.

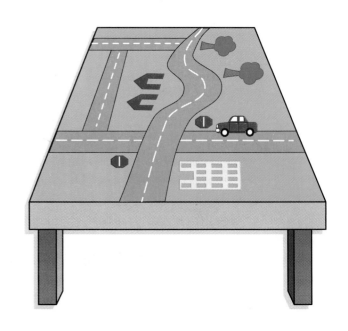

Sharon Otto—Preschool
SRI/St. Elizabeth Child Development Center, Lincoln, NE

Creative Cars

Get your little ones' creative motors running with this zippy idea. Place a toy car on a flat surface; then tape a crayon to the back of the car so that the crayon's tip touches the surface. Invite a child to maneuver the car atop a piece of bulletin board paper to create a unique design.

Michelle West—Three- And Four-Year-Olds
Denton City County Day School
Denton, TX

Come Ride Our Train!

All aboard! Incorporate social studies and art as you take students for an imaginary train ride. Tape lengths of white bulletin-board paper along the walls of a hallway, about a foot off the floor. Draw large rectangles on the paper to distinguish each window on the train. Arrange a carpet square next to each window to provide the seats on the train. Then punch each child's ticket, and let the passengers board. Have a steward serve a snack while children use crayons or markers to draw the scenes they see from their windows! Sing some train songs and read a train story. Then allow each child to tell his address so the train can make an imaginary stop at his house. What a trip!

Donna Selling and Brenda vonSeldeneck—Preschool
First Presbyterian Church
Waynesboro, VA

Keys That Count

Use these Pog® key chains with an assortment of 55 keys to give youngsters practice with counting and number-recognition skills. Label each of 11 Pogs® with a different numeral from 0–10. Punch a hole in each Pog®; then thread one end of a pipe cleaner through the hole and twist to secure as shown. Have a child thread the appropriate number of keys onto the pipe-cleaner portion of each key chain and secure the free end as shown.

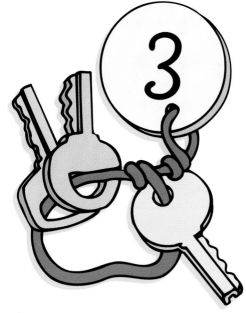

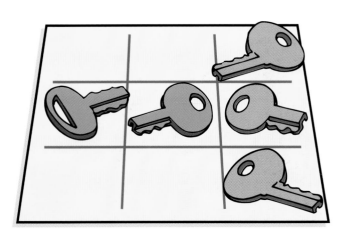

Tic-Tac-Toe Keys

Invite children to use keys as markers in a game of tic-tac-toe. In advance spray-paint ten keys: five red and five blue. To make the gameboard, draw a tic-tac-toe grid on a 12-inch-square sheet of poster board. Laminate the gameboard for durability. To play, each of two players in turn puts a key on the gameboard, attempting to place three of his keys in a row.

Thumbs Up!

These thank-you cards are as unique as thumb-prints themselves. To create a thank-you card for a volunteer or guest, cut out a large card in a shape that relates to the reason for the volunteer's visit. For example, cut an airplane-shaped card for a guest speaker who is a pilot. Write on the card as the class dictates a thank-you message to the volunteer. Have each child press his thumb on an ink pad and then onto the card. Write each child's name under his thumbprint. Thumbs up for these unique thank-you cards!

Donna Leonard—Preschool
Head Start, Dyersville, IA

Reproducible Activities...

Rhyming Wheels
Use these with page 35.

Materials Needed
— crayons or markers
— scissors
— two brads per child

How To Use Pages 34 And 35
1. Duplicate both pages on construction paper for each child. Have each child color her train.
2. Cut out the train along the bold-lines.
3. Cut out the rhyming-picture wheels.
4. Place the rhyming-picture wheels behind the train and attach each wheel with a brad.
5. Have the children turn the wheels until rhyming pictures show in the indentations in the train wheels.

Finished Sample

See You Later, Alligator

Turn the wheels.
Match the rhyming pictures.

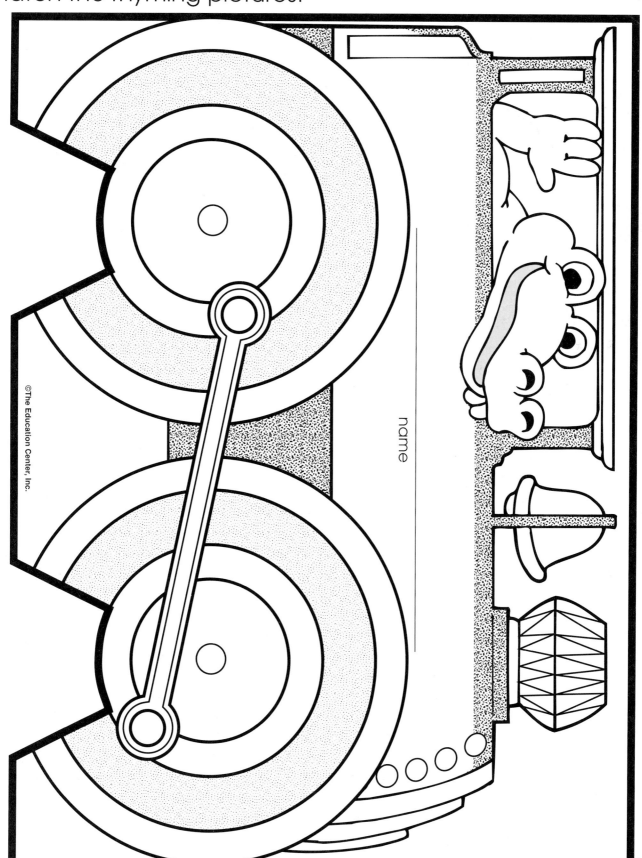

name

How To Use Page 37

1. Introduce the page by reading aloud the poem in the cloud. Help your students imagine a vehicle that could go on the land, on the sea, and in the air. What would it look like? Would it have lights, wings, oars, rockets, wheels, or a combination of the above? Would it have numbers on the side? What color would it be? If you had a vehicle like this, where would you like to go?

2. Encourage the students to trace and finish the drawing by adding details like wheels, wings, etc. In the meantime, assist them with writing their favorite destinations at the bottom of the page.

3. If necessary, staple more manuscript paper to the bottom of the page to increase the writing area.

Finished Sample

Name _____

Vroom! Vroom!

Read.

It can roll!
It can fly!
Over land
And in the sky.

Up and down
On a wave.
You can ride it
If you're brave!

Trace.
Draw.
It looks like this.

Write.
I'd like to go

How To Use Page 39

1. Reproduce the page on construction paper for durability.
2. Cut out the cards and fold them as the instructions direct.
3. Stand the cards up on a table.
4. Arrange the cards by size beginning with the largest and ending with the smallest. Seriate both the boats and the letter *B*s for twice the game fun.
5. Send the cards home in a Ziploc® bag along with a copy of the parent note below for continued learning.

Variation

Reproduce page 39 on regular paper for each child. Cut on both the solid and dotted lines. Provide a 9" x 12" piece of construction paper for each child. The children should seriate the boats by size and glue to the sheet along the 12-inch edge. The children should then seriate the letter *B*s by size, matching them to the corresponding boats, and glue above the boats.

Parent Note

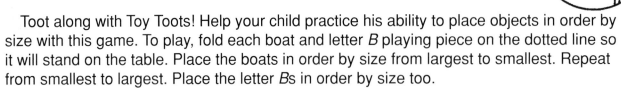

Dear Parent

Toot along with Toy Toots! Help your child practice his ability to place objects in order by size with this game. To play, fold each boat and letter *B* playing piece on the dotted line so it will stand on the table. Place the boats in order by size from largest to smallest. Repeat from smallest to largest. Place the letter *B*s in order by size too.

As your child places the pictures in order, ask him to tell you what he is doing. Use words such as *smaller, smallest, larger,* and *largest*. Extend this game to include objects at home too. Many kitchen utensils are smaller except for size and can be placed in size order. Family socks provide another object to be ordered by size. No matter what the object, talk to your child about size comparisons as often as possible. Doing so will help build necessary vocabulary for reading!

Have fun getting in order by size!

Name _____

Toy Toots

Trace.
Color.

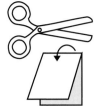

Cut on heavy lines.
Fold on dotted lines.
Put in order by size.

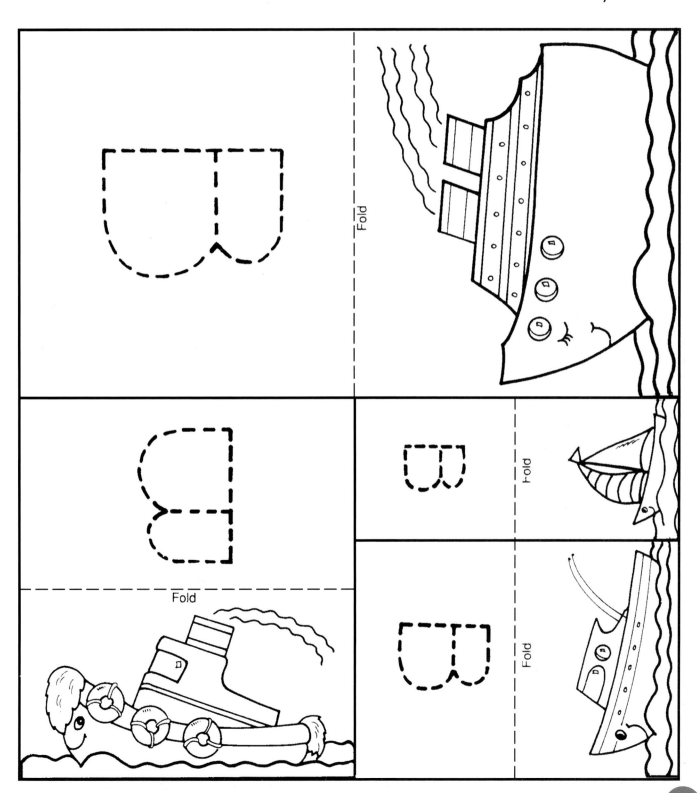

How To Use Page 41

1. Review or read the story *The Little Engine That Could.*
2. Discuss the sequence of the story.
3. Call attention to the pictures at the bottom of page 41. Discuss how they show the sequence of the story. *(First the clown flags down the little engine, then she goes up the mountain, and finally she comes down the mountain.)*
4. Allow independent cutting and gluing to show the sequence of the story.

Extension Activity

Make a sequencing train for extra sequencing practice.

1. Display three 5" x 7" pieces of felt on a flannel board in a horizontal row.
2. Add wheels to the bottom seven-inch edge of each felt rectangle to form the cars of the train.
3. Provide the three-part picture sequence story cards from page 41 with flannel tape on the back.
4. Then have the children arrange the picture cards in order by placing them on the felt train from left to right.
5. Encourage storytelling to go with the correctly sequenced story.

Finished Sample

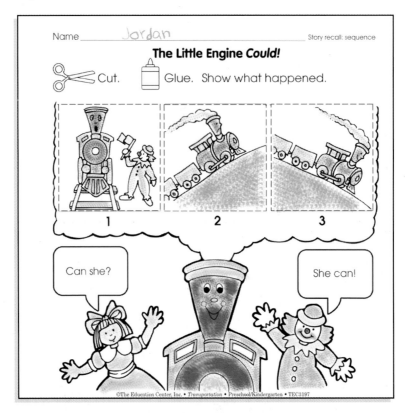

The Little Engine *Could!*

 Cut. Glue. Show what happened.

1	2	3

Can she?

She can!

My Bike Book

Background For The Teacher
Bicycle Safety

Basic bike safety rules for beginners include:

1. Ride one to a bike—no passengers.
2. Keep the bike, especially the brakes, in good repair.
3. Ride during daylight hours only.
4. Keep sturdy shoes on your feet.
5. **Always** wear your bike helmet.

Materials Needed For Each Student

— 1 copy each of pages 43, 45, and 47
— pencil
— crayons
— scissors
— stapler
— 5" piece of string or yarn
— glue

How To Use Page 43
(Booklet Cover And Page 1)

Tell the children that they are going to make a booklet about bike safety. Ask them to share their experiences learning to ride and to relate any bike safety rules that their parents may have taught them. Then help each child follow these directions:

1. Have each child cut out the booklet cover, page 1, and the helmet pattern along the bold lines.
2. Discuss the cover. Read the title. Identify what is happening in the picture. Trace the handlebars. Allow each child to write his name on the line provided. Color the picture.
3. Discuss page 1. Read the sentences at the top of the page. Explain that anyone who rides a bike could get hurt. Let the children relate any tales of crashes that they have experienced. Explain that people sometimes fall on their heads. The head is a bad place to fall, because, unlike elbows or knees, the brain cannot heal itself. Ask if any children have a bike helmet. If possible, have one on hand for the children to inspect and try on. Color Liz and the helmet. Glue the helmet on Liz's head. Ask children to draw Liz's bike in the space provided on the page.
4. Save this booklet page and cover to assemble into the book when all of the pages are complete.

My Bike Book

by _____

Liz rides fast.
She might fall.
She has a helmet.
It keeps her head safe.

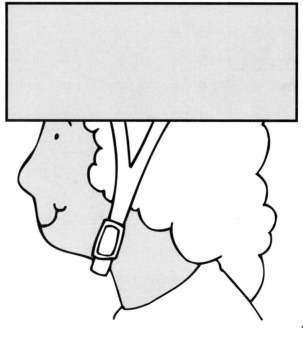

1

How To Use Page 45
(Booklet Pages 2 And 3)

1. Cut off the strip of pictures on the side of the page first. *(The van and bicycle will be used with booklet page 2 and the shoes with booklet page 3.)* Then cut the page into two booklet pages by cutting on the bold lines.

2. Discuss booklet page 2. Identify the scene on the page. Read the sentences. Point out the sidewalk near the bottom of the page. Emphasize the dangers of riding in the street. *(Most accidents involving children occur when they dart out of driveways or from between cars.)* Allow the children to relate any bike safety rules their parents have concerning riding in the street. *(Riding on sidewalks can also be dangerous, and riders should avoid injury to pedestrians, especially smaller children.)* Allow the children to cut the pictures of the van and bicycle from the strip and glue them to page 2 in the appropriate boxes so the bicycle is riding on the sidewalk and the van is driving on the street. Save the page to assemble into the booklet.

3. Discuss booklet page 3. Allow the children to identify the items on the page. Ask what is unusual about each foot. *(They all have injuries.)* Read the sentences to find out why. Help keep the feet from getting hurt again by putting shoes on them. Color and cut apart the shoes on the strip one by one, and glue them over the feet. Save this page to assemble into the booklet.

Finished Sample

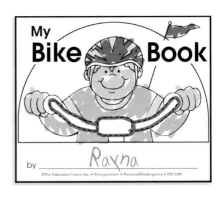

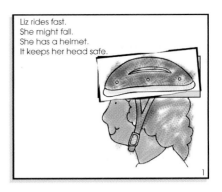

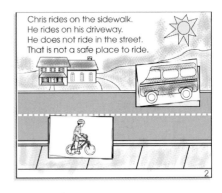

Chris rides on the sidewalk.
He rides on his driveway.
He does not ride in the street.
That is not a safe place to ride.

2

Michelle always rides with her shoes on.
Bare toes can get hurt.
They can slip off the pedals.
Wear shoes that cover your feet.
Sandals are not safe.

3

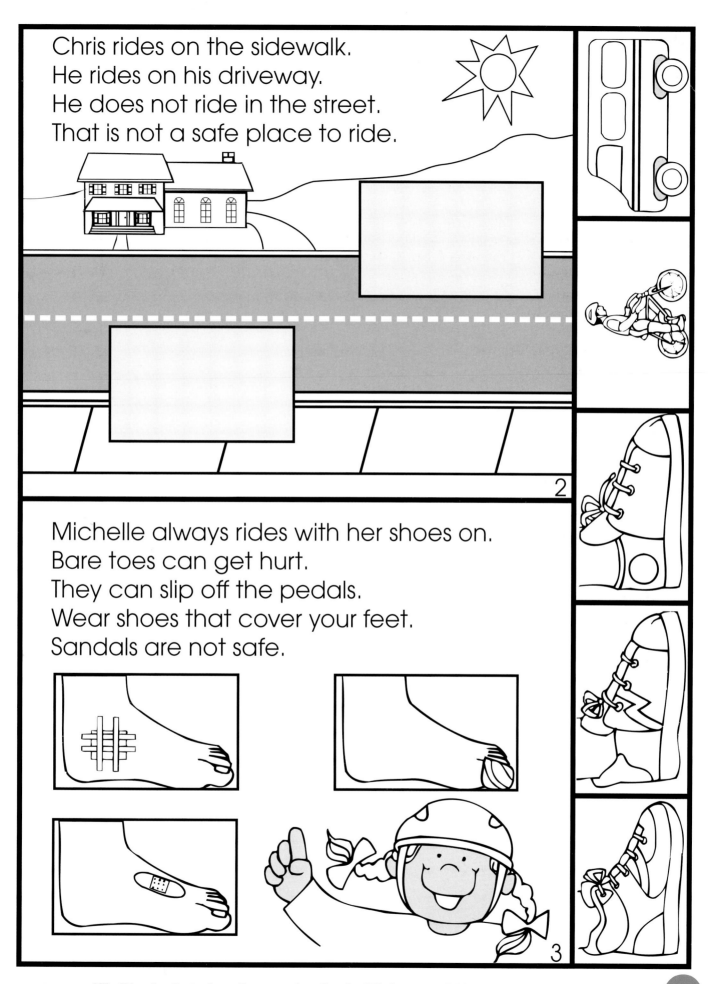

How To Use page 47 (Booklet Pages 4 And 5)

1. Discuss booklet page 4. What is happening in the picture? *(A boy is pumping air into his bike tire.)* Read the sentences together. Have the children trace the wheels on the bike, then color the picture. Next have them glue a piece of yarn to the solid line from the pump to the tire. Save the page to assemble into the booklet.

2. Discuss booklet page 5. What is happening in the picture? *(The girl is putting her bike in the garage because it's dark.)* Read the sentences together. Why is it dangerous to ride at night? *(Decreased vision, shorter reaction time for car drivers, no lights on bikes.)* Have students color the sky to show that it is night. Next have them color and cut apart the stars and moon on the strip. Glue them to the night sky where indicated.

3. Cut out the booklet pages on the bold lines. Then stack the completed pages and staple them behind the cover.

Extension

If possible, have a bike in the classroom and demonstrate how to tell if a tire needs air. Add air to a bike tire with a tire pump. Show how to test the brakes by using the pedals or hand brakes. Identify any reflectors on the bike and discuss their purpose.

Finished Sample

Mike puts air in his tires.
He makes sure his brakes work.
He keeps his bike clean.
A bike that works right is safe to ride.

It is dark.
Lisa puts her bike away.
She does not ride at night.
Tomorrow she will ride again.

Mike puts air in his tires.
He makes sure his brakes work.
He keeps his bike clean.
A bike that works right is safe to ride.

4

It is dark.
Lisa puts her bike away.
She does not ride at night.
Tomorrow she will ride again.

5

Name _____

Hot Wheels Happy

Color the set that shows **more.**

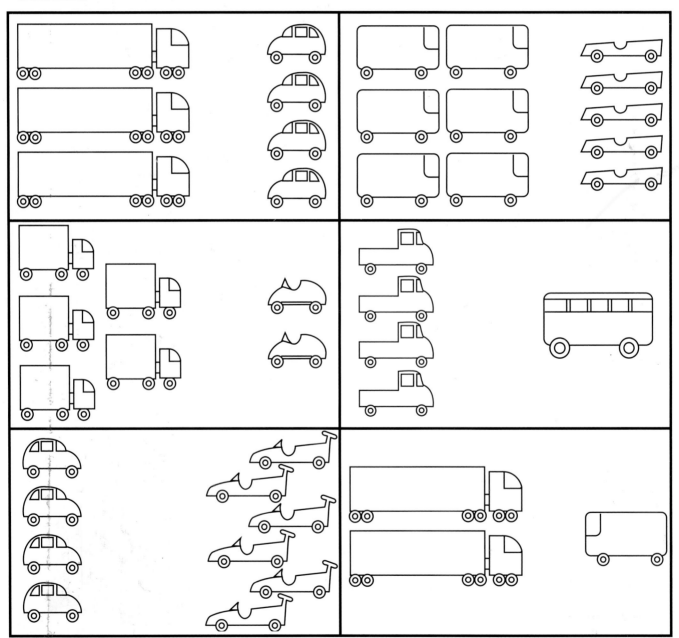

©The Education Center, Inc. • *Transportation* • Preschool/Kindergarten • TEC3197